About the Author

Luke was born in Essex and now lives in London. Helping others is what makes him happiest. This is Luke's debut book. It was inspired from his extensive research into the mind, body and spirit of humans. He wanted to make a profound change to the way he perceived the world. On his journey of self-awareness, he realised there was something that worked best for him. Simply not taking things too seriously, and so the book was born.

LUKE HARDING

50 THINGS

we all take too seriously

AUSTIN MACAULEY PUBLISHERS™

LONDON • CAMBRIDGE • NEW YORK • SHARJAH

A CIP catalogue record for this title is available from the British Library.

ISBN 9781528900201 (Paperback)
ISBN 9781528900218 (E-Book)

www.austinmacauley.com

First Published (2018)
Austin Macauley Publishers™ Ltd.
25 Canada Square
Canary Wharf
London
E14 5LQ

Dedication

I would like to dedicate this book to my mother and father, Jane and Nick Harding. My beautiful and loving mother sadly passed away when I was only three years old. My father should be given a medal for raising many children in very difficult circumstances.
This is for you both!

Acknowledgement

I would like to acknowledge Eckhart Tolle, Mooji, Neil Parkin, Alan Watts, Prince EA, Brian Timoney and Joe Ferriera.
The knowledge and understanding I gained from each of these wonderful people, whether it being in person or through a book, has made me understand myself more than I could ever have imagined.
Thank you!
I would also like to acknowledge Austin Macauley Publishers for taking a chance on me and making this book come to life in order to help many.

Introduction

If you opened this book, then chances are you have been taking life a little too seriously and you should go and sit on the naughty step while you give this a read. Just like you, I used to take life all too seriously and it didn't do me any good. In fact, it made me very unhappy.

Then I went on a 'serious' spiritual journey. I read all the books you should read and watched all the videos you should watch. I went to spiritual events and for a time devoted my life to spiritual teachings in an attempt to become happier. If you have the time, please feel free to do the same. After all, I learnt a lot of very interesting things and can say I am better for it. BUT … if like most people in the modern world, you don't have time for all that, then fear not!

I have compiled my own teachings, based on the most important lesson I learnt of all … NOT TO TAKE LIFE SO BLOODY SERIOUSLY!! In this little book, I will remind you of the ways we all take life way too seriously and how we can change that just by becoming aware that we do so.

Go grab your favourite snack (biscuit, celery stick, I'm not judging) and read the whole thing right now, or open a page a day and give yourself a few minutes for it to sink in. Either way, remember, if you forget to read it one day, it's really not that serious!

There are countless things we worry about day-to-day…
"Have I got any milk in the fridge?"
"Does he/she like me?"
"Am I too fat?"
"Am I too thin?"
"Will I be lonely forever?"
"What happens when I die?"
The list is endless, and when we start to take these things in our lives too seriously, it makes us unhappy! So let me help you with that!

There are 50 unique subjects in this book, each with their own little insight into how we take things too seriously. So, let's get started, but I must warn you … you WILL become less serious and more open, relaxed and playful by the end of this book. So, if that is not something you want, I suggest you post this book through your neighbour's letter-box and run before they realise it was you.
Enjoy!

Luke Harding.

THE BIGGER PICTURE

Our planet is pretty big, right?
WRONG! Although it is too big for any of us to ever
fully explore, it is tiny in comparison to the incredibly,
unimaginably, ginormous UNIVERSE!
There is so much out there which makes our big, green
and blue planet seem actually very small indeed.
Our planet is like a single Rice Krispie within that family-
sized box. Google it, it's unfathomable. So, all the things
you take seriously that cause you stress and make you
unhappy really aren't that serious in the grand scheme.
In the grand scheme, our personal problems don't really
compare to the bigger picture. Just realising this will make
you feel better when things get tough!

THE LOVE LIFE

You can buy them dinner, wear the perfect outfit, try to be
everything you think they would like, impress them with
your best party trick and guess what...
They can still reject you! So, don't take dating so seriously.
Just relax and be yourself, they might just love you for it.
Oh ... and another thing, accept that rejection is a part of
life and not something to be taken seriously. MOVE ON!
The right one for you might just be waiting around the
corner. Be your true self and eventually someone will love
you for it.
There are so many fish in the sea. A fair few of them are
perfectly compatible with you. It just so happens that you
haven't crossed paths yet. The good news is, YOU WILL!
And if you already have, don't forget to treat your fish well!

LET GO

Wouldn't it be great if we could point a remote control at someone and command them to do something, and they would just do it! Such things as:

"Give me a promotion."

"Be attracted to me."

"Choose me for your next Hollywood movie."

"Go and get me a chocolate bar from the shop."

That would be great, right? Well, unfortunately, that is not how it works. So many situations are completely out of your control, so you are better off relaxing and letting go of the need for control. Go with the flow and take your need for control less seriously.

YOU ARE WHAT YOU EAT

Now this isn't an obvious one, because to a degree, you need a bit of seriousness when it comes to your diet. After all, we all know deep down that we need to eat our fair share of broccoli and berries in order to feel our best and look after our bodies inside and out. Our health is, arguably, the most important thing to us.

Yet there is such a thing as too serious a diet. Food is such a joy of life and to deny certain things completely that you really enjoy, because of your diet, is no fun at all. So, if you are serious about your diet and tell yourself you are a bad person for eating that Mars bar, then give yourself a break. Be a bit naughty and think about potentially taking your diet less seriously. Alternatively, if you eat no fruit or veg, it might well be time to start. Good health can really improve your happiness.

ACCEPTANCE

It's 8:30 am and you are stuck in a serious traffic jam.
There is no way you are going to make it into work by
9:00am. Your mind begins to go bonkers:
"Everyone is going to look at me judgmentally, again."
"My boss is going to be in a bad mood with me all day."
"I will have to stay late."
"I could lose my job."
"If I lose my job, my girlfriend will leave me."
You can spend the rest of the journey stressing yourself
out and worrying about all of these things OR you can
accept that there is no way to change this, blast your
favourite song while you wait and not take an
unchangeable situation so seriously.

EXERCISE

Just like your diet, a little seriousness in exercise is something that you can benefit from greatly in life. Anyone who exercises regularly knows you feel great after getting a decent sweat on a few times a week. It reduces stress and increases energy. So, getting your running shoes on is something to be taken seriously if you want a healthier life.

BUT ... (there's that 'but' again), exercise should not be a chore. If you find yourself lifting weights just to get the girl, or running for miles even though you despise it, does it really make you happy? Be a little less serious with your exercise and make sure you are doing it for the right reasons. If you are bored of it, then find another way. I highly recommend squash! And if you are doing it just for image, think about how much you rely on your image ... which brings me to my next point.

ME, MYSELF AND I

Some of us beat ourselves up way too often. We look at ourselves and see the negatives, the things we don't like. Then we go to great lengths to correct it, or we battle against it every time we look in the mirror. Whether your teeth are slightly wonky or you aren't quite the weight you want to be. You look at yourself and say,
"NO I DON'T ACCEPT THAT."
It doesn't have to be that way though. If we could relax and be less serious about what we look like, what might happen? Well we might say, "YES I ACCEPT THAT," when we look in the mirror.
How refreshing would that be? To be content with yourself fully. Can you imagine the relief?
Well, you can do it right now just by accepting yourself and not taking your image so seriously. Go to your nearest mirror and give it a try. Smile at the reflection and notice how it smiles back at you.

EXPRESS YOURSELF

You are at a wedding and the DJ starts playing a bit of Michael Jackson. Your feet start tapping, but you are not a dancer. *You never dance, everyone knows that. If you were the first one to get up and dance, what would your family and friends think? They might think you've gone insane or that you are drunk.*

How about stopping this mind chatter, taking yourself less seriously, following that feet tap and letting the music course through your veins. Get on that dance floor and show them what you've got, superstar!

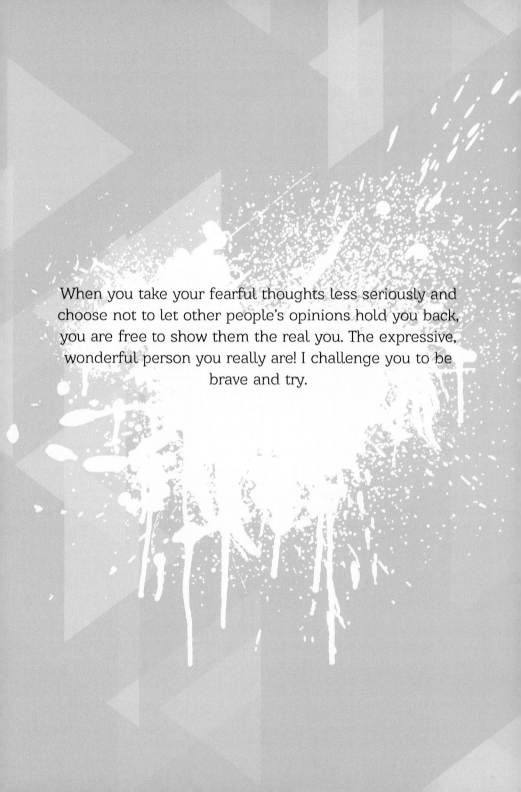

When you take your fearful thoughts less seriously and choose not to let other people's opinions hold you back, you are free to show them the real you. The expressive, wonderful person you really are! I challenge you to be brave and try.

FACE YOUR FEAR

Fear, fear, fear! That little bugger. Heights, spiders, bees, snakes, other humans, baked beans (I once met a girl who was terrified of baked beans). These fears are imbedded in our mind and can be hard to get over.

Then you have anxiety. A whole other level of fear. It can consume your entire life if you let it.

The future scares us because it cannot be predicted and is out of our control, and as we have already spoken about, we love to be in control. Fear creates stress and that makes us unhappy. I'm not saying fear will be easy to take less seriously, but I ask you to test fear. If you are scared of spiders, try being calmer next time you see one. If you are anxious, just remind yourself that the future is not real, it's just in your mind and you shouldn't take that too seriously. And speaking of the mind, the next page explains why our mind can get the better of us.

THE MIND

The human mind is so powerful. We can access memories and information from our earliest years. We solve complex problems and we create amazing things. We couldn't do any of it without the mind. Yet with great power comes great responsibility.

In this sense, the responsibility is to keep your mind in check. Yes, it helps us through life, but it also has the ability to make our lives miserable.

Try not taking your mind so seriously. When you believe everything that the mind is telling you, then it has control over you and can make you unhappy. The opposite is the truth. You have control over your thoughts and have the power to change them.

So next time your mind starts racing about terrible things, become aware. Say, "I'm okay right now," and just take your thoughts less seriously!

THE WEATHER

You wake up mid-June, you look outside and it is grey and rainy. You instantly slump and tell yourself it's going to be a rubbish day.

It's fair to say the weather can really affect our mood! BUT ... it doesn't have to. When we take our normal perceptions of the weather too seriously, we set ourselves up for negativity when it's not what we want it to be.

What if we could choose to go against the grain though? Perhaps the next time it rains and you look outside, you can thank your lucky stars that the air is going to get a good clean and the plants a good water.

Don't take the weather too seriously, it will just ruin your day!

PLAY MORE

By now, you can begin to understand that there are many ways to take life less seriously, and how it can make you a happier person. Once this realisation kicks in, something quite marvellous happens. You begin to see that life doesn't have to be such a drag and a struggle anymore. You stop looking upon things as a means to an end and you start to relax around so-called stressful tasks, because now you know that they don't really matter as much as you once thought they did.

When you take this more relaxed approach to life, you also begin to PLAY more. You know life isn't all that serious and you start to laugh at it and have fun with it. You are free to release your inner child again.

AGE

When we get to certain ages, society tells us we should behave a certain way. Suddenly, we play less than we used to as a kid, become a model citizen, behave 'properly' in public, think about our future more etc.

Now it's safe to say some of these things are important. If we didn't grow up, then how would we achieve anything? We would still be playing in the sandbox and riding round on our bikes all day.

Age does bring responsibility, there is no doubt ... BUT, why not bring out that inner child sometimes. Be silly in public, play more (as we just discussed) and don't grow up too much!

MONEY, MONEY, MONEY

We all have our own personal issues to deal with, and they
usually stem from childhood. My biggest issue to work on
has been money. I used to take it way too seriously.
I was uncomfortable with spending it. It probably sounds
silly to many of you, but this issue stems back from my
childhood. For a big part of it, we had really bad money
problems and I spent a long time hearing about how we
can't afford this or that.
Now, sometimes we need to think about our money.
Saving for something really nice is a great thing to do and
knowing when you literally can't afford something is wise.
BUT ... money comes and goes, and as they say, "You gotta
spend money to make money." So, if you are like me and
take money way too seriously, then just DON'T.
Be wise with your money but don't let it hold you back.
When you spend it in the right way, you might just get
more back.

THE PAST

This one won't apply to everyone. Every person has a different mentality. Some of us never think about the past, some rarely think about the future and some don't think much at all. They just live in the moment.

I personally rarely think about the past and have taught myself to think about the future less. What about you? The past has already been and gone. It can now only exist in your mind. In reality, it doesn't exist anymore.

So if you are someone who finds it hard to let go of certain events in your past, just realising this will help set you free from it.

Try taking the past less seriously. Let go of it. Who you are right now has nothing to do with who you were yesterday or ten years ago.

THE FUTURE

The twin sister of the past, a.k.a. the FUTURE!
The places we will go, the things we will achieve or fail at,
the great unknown, the fantasies of what could be.
Just like the past, the future doesn't exist. The past no
longer exists, but the future has never existed. How can it
when it is yet to happen.
BUT ... we love to think about it. We love to imagine what
might happen, whether it's good or bad. Sometimes, the
future is a scary horrible place we are not looking forward
to; also known as anxiety. Then there is the opposite,
otherwise known as anticipation; where the thoughts of the
future create excitement in us.
Guess what ... both are actually a little bit INSANE! It's
all an illusion of the mind. Okay, so sometimes it is very
helpful to plan ahead and have goals, but don't forget,
even that isn't real. So be less serious about the future and
instead enjoy NOW.

SLOW DOWN

Have you ever heard the expression 'slow and steady wins the race?' If you haven't, your special task is to read the short story 'Tortoise and the Hare'. It has a great message behind it.

In the western world, we live life mostly in the fifth gear. We are always busy. There is always something we need to do, or forgot to do, or have no time to do and it makes us busy little bees. So busy, in fact, that we begin to get ourselves worked up and cause ourselves stress. It seems like the list is never-ending. We all have things that we have been meaning to do but just don't have the time. The lesson here is to SLOW DOWN. What's all the rush? When we rush, we don't give individual tasks care and attention which only creates more problems. Don't think of all the things you need to do. Think of the one thing you can do NOW and slow down and concentrate on it.

Go from fifth gear to second, more often.

SWEET NOTHING

There is no better way to slow down than to do literally nothing. Take some time out from your serious schedule once in a while, go to your favourite spot and just sit there and do sweet nothing.

Just sit there and sink into the moment. Switch off your brain and just settle yourself into your surroundings. Look around you and don't judge or label what you see. Just take it all in and be with it.

You might notice a strange sense of calm wash over you. You are officially slowing down!

Doing nothing every now and then will make you take life less seriously, because you begin to realise you have everything you could possibly need right there in that moment.

ILLNESS

It's quite extraordinary how hard our body works to keep us in one piece. We don't always do the best things for it, but it always perseveres and keeps on functioning. We should not take for granted the fact that we are kept alive every day by the complex inner mechanics which occur inside our bodies. It's another one worth googling, because it will make you aware of how impressive the human body really is.

BUT ... things do go wrong sometimes. It could be a simple cold, or it could be a life-threatening disease. Either way, it reminds us of how much we want to be healthy again and we must trust that our body is doing everything it can to make that happen.

My point here is to not see illness as an unwelcomed guest, but welcome it until it decides to leave when it is ready.

AMBITIONS

This is another one I throw my own hands up to and say, "I am guilty of taking my ambitions too seriously." I'm going to go and sit on the naughty step while I write this. It's great to have an ambition. It's an attractive trait and is the route to success. Without it, we wouldn't achieve very much at all. You might be thinking what could possibly be wrong with ambition?

Well, I know first-hand that if it is taken too seriously, it can make you unhappy. When you have a fixed ambition, you put all your eggs in one basket and when that basket gets knocked over (in other words, you fail), it can hurt. This seems pretty normal, but it doesn't have to be that way. You can spread a couple of eggs elsewhere or you can accept and understand that your basket is going to take many a knock and be cool with that. Ambition is your friend, but don't take your relationship with it too seriously. Which nicely leads me to the next page.

RELATIONSHIPS

Depending on who we are with can often make us adapt how we act. For example, you act differently around your dad in comparison to how you act around your best friend. Your teacher will see a different side to you compared to the one your boyfriend or girlfriend sees when you are both alone together. This is pretty normal and expected. YET ... sometimes we take our roles within a relationship a little too seriously. We can get into a habit of moulding ourselves into a shape that pleases the person we are with. The way we talk to our parents may be less expressive than what we are really feeling or wanting to say. We may avoid saying certain things or doing certain things such as farting in bed, to please our partner. BUT ... this isn't showing our full selves. You can break the mould whenever you like just by taking the way you approach a particular relationship less seriously and by being the full, crazy, weird person that you are.

SOCIETY

We don't just play roles in relationships. We also play them every day when we go into society.

It's easy to slip into professional 'phone voice' when we talk to someone we don't know on the phone. It's also easy to treat your waiter very differently to the people you are with at the restaurant. The way we talk to children and elderly would be seen as condescending if it was spoken to another adult.

So, why do we do it? Well, somewhere along the way, we get a little detached from humanity. We forget that all humans are made the same and that we are in this together. We change our act based on the superiority or inferiority of the other person.

BUT ... it doesn't have to be that way. I have made it my mission to talk to every human being the same way and with the same amount of respect that they show me. I challenge you to do the same if you don't already. You become much more relatable when you do this. Consider the roles of society as a less serious concept and see the humanity in everyone.

DEATH

I know what you are thinking ... "Is he really going to bring me down by reminding me that I'm, one day, going to die?" Well ... Yes, that's what I am doing, but not with the intention of bringing you down. In fact, quite the opposite. Death is something we have the odd joke about but isn't something we often like to talk about. We all know deep down it will happen and we know countless ways it could happen. It is VERY SCARY, no one can deny that.

BUT ... it doesn't have to be that way. If you can sit down and really accept death is coming, it can actually be quite liberating. When I wake up in the morning, I try and remind myself that there are 100 ways I could die today. Look it up, there really are! It instantly makes me appreciate my day ahead.

By accepting death will happen, we don't see it as a threat and therefore take it less seriously. Suddenly, we aren't so scared of death anymore.

SELF-ESTEEM

We have already discussed how we can take the things we don't like about ourselves too seriously. I want to go more in-depth into this as it is such a big cause of pain and unhappiness among us humans.

You may have heard the saying about how you need to learn to love yourself before loving someone else. I fully believe this to be a good way to do things. When we bring all of our insecurities and lack of self-esteem into a relationship, it's hard to relax and be yourself. When we carry it all around with us without facing up to it, it can have an effect on us in every situation. The real us doesn't shine through.

I challenge you to confront your biggest insecurities. Is it your appearance? If so, change it, or truly accept it the way it is. You were given the body you are in and you have control over how it is maintained. You don't have control over its features. SO ... you can either look at it negatively, or not take it so seriously and be happy with who you are. It really is just a choice.

WHAT OTHERS THINK

This one will truly change your life if you can put it into action. We have all been guilty, at one time or another, of taking what others think of us way too seriously.

Say you are on the train and your favourite song comes on your iPod and all you want to do is sing along to it, but you are worried about what everyone around you might think. Most of us would shy away from going through with singing. BUT ... perhaps you can remember that person you thought was a bit crazy who was doing just this. Well, I must tell you that they were either drunk, or probably much less serious than you are. They didn't care what others thought; they expressed how they felt they really wanted to at that time.

When we stop caring what others think, we let our true selves shine through. We aren't held down by society and other people's judgements because we really don't care. We just want to have fun. When you are doing this, you are giving the middle finger to seriousness.

PEOPLE PLEASING

Linking very closely to the last page, some of us aim to please others because we are very conscious of what they think of us. The irony here is that by trying to please someone, you can actually annoy them. We all know that one person who never disagrees with you and who is just overly nice, and it always make us a little uncomfortable. If you think this might be you, this is a hugely valuable lesson for you.

We like genuine people, it's such an attractive trait. Saying what you truly feel, despite the circumstances, is not only brave but also honest. People-pleasers will say and do what they think people want them to. They choose to hold back their actual opinions.

Although you have the other person's best interest here, it makes you weak and not genuine.

Instead, next time someone does something that annoys you, or you strongly disagree with their opinion, then challenge it. You don't have to be mean about it, you just say what you feel and you may find you actually gain some respect. Take your need to please people far less seriously.

JUDGEMENT

Humans are judgmental creatures. Apparently, we make a full judgement on someone in just nine seconds. That's all it takes for us to decide how we think another person might be like. Sometimes we are right, most of the time we are wrong.

The challenge of the day is to not take your judgements so seriously. When you look at someone you don't know, try not to make up your mind about them and who they are without giving a bit of time to actually get to know them. I'm not saying you should get to know everyone you lay eyes on, that just isn't possible.

What I'm saying is if you don't know them, then never assume something about them.

Perhaps an example is in order. You see a scruffy man walk past you on the street with no shoes. You assume he is homeless and a waste of space and ignore him and look down on him. Little do you know, the man cares little for appearance, is actually a millionaire and just gave his shoes to someone more in need. Okay, that's a crazy example, but still completely possible. Try not to judge until you know more.

EGO

We all have an ego! Some are big, some are small. Our ego is basically that voice in our head which tells us who we are. It says things like:

"You are great."

"You are worthless."

"Nobody loves you."

"Everybody loves you."

"You are so good looking."

"You are ugly."

These are all lies which your mind tells you! The truth is, our ego isn't us at all. It is purely what we trick ourselves into believing we are. This might be hard to grasp so let me explain.

When you think you are superior to someone, that's your ego talking. The same when you think you are inferior. If we lived in a world where everyone saw each other as equal, then there would be no ego. This would make room for love to shine through. So, how about trying to take your ego less seriously.

EGO – PART 2

I believe the ego is a fairly complicated thing to grasp, but a valuable lesson, so I would like to continue on this point. Hope you don't mind. This is one of the more serious topics in a pretty altogether-unserious book.

Let me explain how my ego used to work. I used to think it was really unfair that other people were happier than I was, that they were richer than I was. I felt inferior. I wanted to show I was worthy. So, when I did something cool, I would show it to the world and I would carry that past glory around with me time and again as I showed it off. As I achieved things, I would love talking about them and believed I was better than others because of my achievements. Little did I know this was my ego at work. BUT ... then I learnt that what I'd done and who I thought I was based on my successes and failures wasn't really me. I realised we are all equal. Whether the president or a homeless man, we are all the same and that was a huge lesson for me. My ego was telling me I was better. It made me into a more self-centred person. Now it doesn't have control over me; I am more loving. Do you feel inferior or superior in life?

THAT IS YOUR EGO!

SOCIETY – PART 2

All this ego talk leads us nicely onto my next point. We have already discussed the roles we play within society and how we can take them a bit seriously.

I want to look at that again but this time in regards to being superior or inferior.

Let's start with 'superior'. You are walking down the street and you see a homeless man begging for money. Now, in society, this is seen as the lowest of the low. Many of us will have looked at this person and felt a sense of superiority. There's that ego creeping in again. In truth, that man is equal. Neither inferior nor superior. It just so happens he hasn't had it as easy.

So, perhaps we can show him some humanity and love and give him a coin or two. Now for 'inferior'. You are called to your boss's office. You get ready to be super polite and very nice to them; you feel threatened by them. Before you have even gotten into the office, you have told yourself you are inferior. BUT ... why not try seeing him as equal to you and talk to him in such a way? See what happens then.

TO-DO LIST

Let's face it, these lists are quite often things we don't really want to do. We do them because we have certain responsibilities to uphold, both to ourselves and others.

1.   Do the laundry.
2.   Write 'thank you' cards.
3.   Send off all invoices.
4.   Buy food from the supermarket.
5.   Book trains for the weekend.

The list can go on. It's great to take responsibility for life, but NOT when it begins to make you unhappy. Sometimes the list seems endless and the entire day feels like one big chore.
Here's the good news. If you complete the most important two on the list and the others don't quite get done, well guess what? There is always tomorrow. Try not taking your to-do list too seriously. If you feel like you have had enough for today, get the kettle, put your feet up and make that "AHHH" noise.

HOLDING GRUDGES

You've had a huge argument with your best friend. You were going to order pizza. He wanted pepperoni, but you hate pepperoni. You say you are happy to have anything else, but he refuses. The easy solution is just to get two smaller sizes of each, but it's too late. You are now both in a full-blown argument. You say he is selfish, he says you are too fussy. It escalates rapidly and next thing you know, you storm out of his house and all the way home.

You both think you are right and end up not talking for a week. Stubbornness takes over and gets right in the way of your friendship.

Then one of you buys my book and reads this: "IT'S A SLICE OF PIZZA, WHY SO SERIOUS?" You realise the entire argument was ridiculous and really not that serious in comparison to your friendship. It is clear now that holding this grudge is just plain silly and you go around to your friend's house and say, "Shall we forgive and forget?" The grudge is lifted and your friendship returns. This is one silly example of how utterly pointless grudges are. Not something to be taken seriously.

PROBLEMS

A problem is an unwelcomed guest that unfolds at some point in our day. It causes us stress as we say, "WHY IS THIS HAPPENING? GRRR." We always find a way to solve it, but it can ruin our day if we let it.

What about if we didn't let it though?

Next time you get a flat tyre, or you find out you went way over your phone bill, why not choose to take to it less seriously? It's still not a desirable situation, but because it is now less serious to you, you don't stress yourself out over it. You stay calm, clearly think of the solution and go about solving it. You take pride in solving it in such a calm manner and probably do so sooner because you have a level head.

So next time a so-called 'problem' occurs, just accept it. Maybe even laugh at it and by doing so, you automatically take it far less seriously.

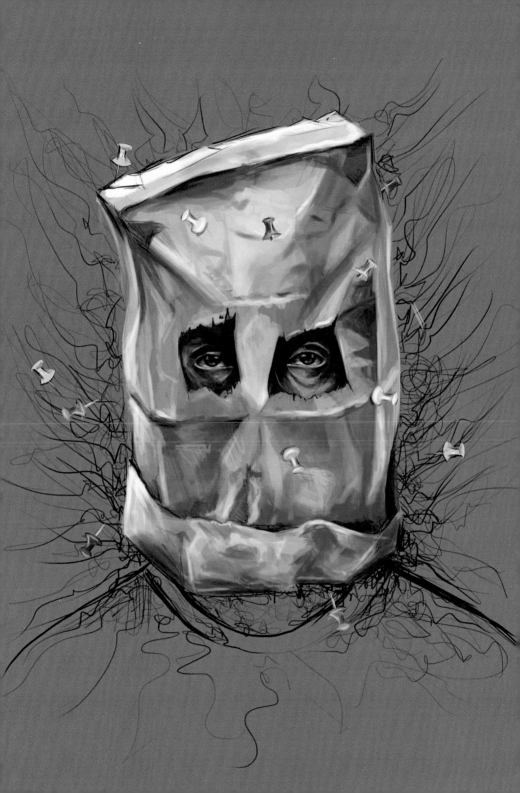

BE GRATEFUL

Another great way to make our own little problems seem
less serious is to be more grateful.
Think about how lucky you are.
Firstly, you were born. You managed to beat all of the
other individual and unique little sperms in the ultimate
race, even before you saw the light of day. Even that can
be enough to make you grateful.
Chances are you can afford to eat every day, have a bed to
sleep in and a roof over your head. There are millions in
this world who do not have even these simple necessities.
How about the opportunities you have? We are lucky
enough to be able to be anything we want to, if we work
hard enough and put enough effort in. Yet, in some parts
of the world, these opportunities that we are privileged
with are not at all a possibility. Many children don't even
have access to education. An automatic lack of opportunity.
So next time your flat tyre or phone bill makes you sad,
think of all that you have to be grateful for.

MAN AND WOMAN

Men and women are equal. Think about it, humanity would not survive without both of us being around. We need the sperm and the egg. Therefore, we are both as valuable as each other to our existence.

YET ... as we know from history, and also still in the present day, there are many men and women who fail to see this. Throughout the history books, there are stories of men abusing and trying to control women; acts of fear and selfishness and a lack of love. Some men still don't see women as there equals and this is very sad. There are women in the world also guilty of this narrow view. Extreme feminism puts all men in the same category based on the wrong doings of one, or a few men, in the woman's life; equally narrow-minded. There are plenty of good-hearted, compassionate men in the world. Men and women who believe they are superior to the opposite sex could do with sitting on the serious naughty step and realising that they take their gender too seriously.

TIME

"What's the time?" Your friend asks in the middle of a really fun board game that you and your best friends have become lost in. You have completely forgotten that time even exists because you are too busy having fun. You are not aware that there will be an ending, you are just enjoying being with people you love and having a good time with them. Then this joyful, timeless spell gets broken with that question, "What's the time?" Suddenly, everybody becomes aware of time again and begins to think about their own personal futures.

"Oh no, it's getting late, I've got to be up in the morning." Of course, it's often important to know the time. We do need it in our lives to function well, but wouldn't it be nice to be concerned with it as little as possible? Perhaps this person was up really early and needed to leave by 10:00 pm. That's fair enough, but if they spend the entire night worried about the time, then they lose the moment. They basically take time too seriously. Next time they go to their friend's house, they could set an alarm for 10:00pm, forget all about time and have a great evening.

CHANGE

Change is a part of life and quite often comes without our permission. Sometimes the changes can be small, like a change of schools or going grey or bald. Then, other times, they can be big. Like an unexpected pregnancy, a sudden change in your career or even a life-threatening illness that has come out of nowhere.

We don't ask for these things, yet they arrive on us like a ton of bricks. There are two ways of dealing with this, resisting it or adapting to your new situation. When we resist we say, "NO" to our situation which makes us unhappy. When we adapt, we say, "OKAY, I will roll with this." Think of evolution. None of us would be here if our primate ancestors said no to adapting to their situations. They wouldn't have survived without great adaptive skills.

So if the monkeys can do it, so can we. Next time something changes, don't take it so seriously, just go with the new flow you have been given.

THE LOVE LIFE PART 2

We discussed briefly, how relaxing and being yourself around somebody you want to be with, or are already with, is the best road to go down. When you pretend to be something that you are not, the truth will always come out eventually. We tend to think that we have to be a certain way to attract the opposite sex.

Men will try and impress the girl with how cool and successful they are or how big their biceps are. Any girl will tell you this is NOT attractive. She wants to feel comfortable around you, she wants to laugh with you (and not take things seriously) and she wants to feel your sexuality. And really, all you have to do is have the courage to show these parts of yourself as they are for you as an individual. Not how you think they should be. We all have the ability to feel our individual sexuality.

Women, from a man's perspective, the more real and genuine you are, the more we like you. Don't be afraid to show us who you really are. You also have your own individual sexuality and if you want to show it and tell a man how you feel, we respect that. Don't take the love life seriously, just be yourself!

PLANNING

We have already discussed the future, and how it is really an illusion and not real in this moment. Yet, it is sometimes useful to think ahead and to plan. To set out a plan is to follow a set of steps which you hope will lead to a successful ending in whatever you are trying to achieve. Each step should bring you a step closer as you begin to work towards it while following your plan.

BUT ... plans also have a huge flaw. They are always based on the future and are, therefore, unaware of the journey you will take between steps. So much changes on your journey. You learn as you go and soon your original plan is almost non-existent. The only thing that stays the same is the end goal.

There's nothing wrong with a plan, but don't take it too seriously. Be willing to adapt to whatever is thrown at you. Focus all your energy into each step without any expectation of even getting to the end goal.

Because the step you are taking right now is the only real thing at the moment.

WHY SO SERIOUS?

Most of you will have heard of 'The Joker'. If you haven't, he is a fictional character from 'The Batman' stories. He is famous for being a complete maniac.

He causes unmotivated and pointless chaos in Gotham City time and again. He laughs at the world around him as it sinks into demise.

You are probably wondering what this has to do with not being serious? Well, there is a lesson to be learnt from this maniac. The lesson is definitely not to cause chaos, but rather to laugh at the world around you. Ideally, in a not so evil way. After all, nobody likes evil people.

When you can find humour in the world that surrounds you, it instantly makes you very unserious.

I find myself laughing at the silliest things, but it brings me much joy. What can you find humour in today that you usually would not?

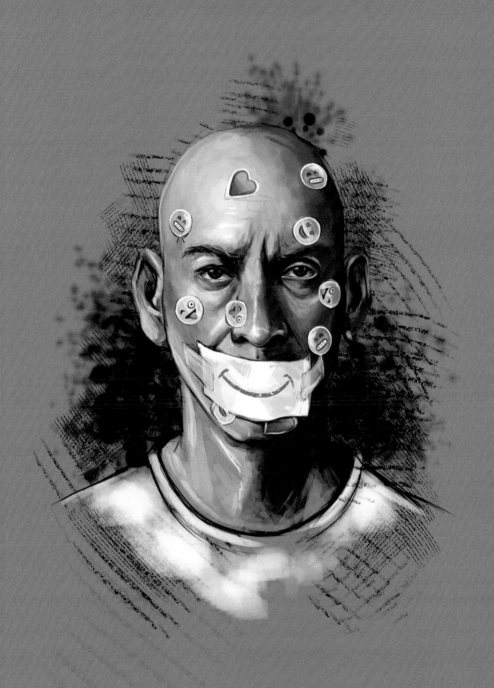

THE MIND – PART 2

As we have already discussed, our mind is very powerful.
So much so, that it can be a burden to us if we let it.
Over-thinking is a hard habit to break. If you are used to
thinking long and hard about the past, present or future
situations, then it can seem impossible to switch your brain
off. You might sometimes catch yourself in deep thought
and wonder 'why' after snapping out of it. Yet, before long,
another thought takes up your energy and time.
So many thoughts pass through our heads, some of which
can really get us down in the dumps.
The good news is that there is an easy cure to over-
thinking. It's called 'THE SERIOUS ANTIDOTE'. All you have
to do is first become aware you are actually thinking about
something way too much. Then you take that thought and
you imagine injecting it with 'THE
SERIOUS ANTIDOTE' and say, "This thought is not
so serious after all." When you give a thought less
seriousness, it becomes less important, and before you
know it, it has faded away. It may return, but just repeat
the process.

THE BIGGER PICTURE PART 2

At the very start of the book, we spoke briefly about how small we really are, and how it makes our problems seem less serious by realising this.

Well, just for the fun of it, I would like to introduce another profound thought which always reminds me how unserious my silly little problems are.

In this unfathomable universe, we are yet to discover any other life forms away from our own home planet. Based on this fact, it is still unknown whether we are all alone on this ginormous universe, or whether there are other species out there somewhere. Both of these possibilities, when you really think about it, are truly fascinating.

We are so small, yet what if we are the only ones in all of space and time?

Or if there is something out there, what do they look like? Would they like us? Will we ever meet them?

I find thinking about the bigger picture is a great way to get out of your own serious and small life.

Try it out. Look up.

RIGHT AND WRONG

There are some things that are clearly right. It's clearly right to help others and to support those in need. It's clearly right to do something nice for another person. There are also things that are clearly wrong. It's clearly wrong to murder another human being. It's clearly wrong to steal from another. These are wrong because they destroy peace and harmony, and as is easy to imagine a murderous world where everyone steals from one another would not be a very pleasant place to live.

BUT ... what about the things that are less obviously right or wrong?

Say, for example, speeding in your car on your way to the hospital with your pregnant wife in the back. Now, the other cars with people who take life too seriously in, would huff and puff and say, "How irresponsible, that is clearly wrong!" Well, I wonder if they knew what was happening in the car, whether they would change their minds? Right and wrong isn't always clear-cut. Blurring the boundaries is far less serious and far more exciting.

OPINION

We all know that person who always thinks they are right and will not admit when they are wrong. It's as if they will argue there point all the way to the grave.
SERIOUS ALERT! This person is very serious. We all have an opinion and sometimes our opinion is deemed worthy by others. If this is the case everything is sunshine and rainbows. BUT ... the opposite can turn the seemingly nicest, laid-back people into a huge ball of seriousness mixed with aggression and stubbornness. When our opinion is challenged, we can take it as a personal threat. If we are really serious about our opinion, we may even start to raise our voices. We may feel hatred towards the other person. Can you understand how this makes us suddenly very serious? The alternative is to either try and understand the other point of view, or even make a joke about your differences.
Personal opinions can easily be taken way too seriously. If you think this could be you, perhaps you could try releasing the grip on your opinions a bit?

OTHER PEOPLE'S OPINION

It is equally as relieving not to take other people's opinion of you so seriously. We have already discussed not caring too much about what people think of you.

This next point ties in with that.

People will always have an opinion of you. You could be the nicest, best-looking, most respectful person to ever walk this earth, and yet some people will try and create a bad opinion of you. The way we view other people is a great reflection of ourselves. If we look for the good in others, chances are we look for the good in ourselves, and it works just the same with the bad. This, in itself, should make you realise that someone else's opinion of you isn't to be taken seriously. It's usually to do with their own problems. Chances are they view many people in this bad light they have created for you.

I mean, if you do horrible things, then you deserve it and should try and be better, but if not, then just choose not to take other people's opinion of you so seriously.

HUMANS AND ANIMALS

It's sometimes easy to forget that we are just another animal on this planet. It just so happens that we are the most intelligent and forward-thinking. This is the sole reason why we are top of the food chain. If it was down to just strength, I'm sure the lions or bears would win. If it was down to speed, the cheetahs or rabbits would win. What about size? Well, we all know we wouldn't win that one. Fortunately for us though, intelligence is the most powerful attribute we can have. Evident from the power we have on this planet.

BUT ... we shouldn't forget how we are just another animal on this planet. With all our power, surely we have a responsibility to our fellow animals? Yet, we abuse our power and take it way too seriously. We forget that we are all in this together. Mammals, birds, reptiles, insects, we are all one, made up of the same atoms and molecules. I'm not saying we should all become vegans, but let's perhaps take our own power as humans less seriously and use it for good in regards to our fellow animals.

CULTURE

There are so many cultures on this earth. Each one can teach us a little something. In our western culture, we have many benefits. We ensure everybody is given the opportunity to an education, we make sure everybody is treated medically in times of need and the majority of mouths are fed daily. BUT ... we also have our downfalls. There is a certain amount of selfishness and seriousness in our culture. It's as if most of us are on a one-man mission to live the lives we want. Sometimes we lack a sense of community, generally (not always).

Let's look at Africa now. We have all seen the poverty that is there. A lack of opportunity, a lack of food and a lack of medical care. Many have it pretty tough! Yet anyone who has been to Africa and met the locals will have seen what a fantastic sense of community they have. They are grateful for the little they have and help one another. They sing together to bring joy into a difficult life.

They aren't very serious.

This is just one example of quite different cultures and each has its own lessons on how to be less serious. So, spread your wings and learn about other cultures if you have the time.

CLASS

We have friends who are richer than us, and friends who are poorer than us.
BUT ... middle class, lower class and upper class, do we really all get on when friendship isn't involved?
I find this can often not be the case. It's inevitable, if you are upper class, that you will probably live in an upper-class area and go to an upper-class school and generally be surrounded by upper-class people. So, it's no surprise that most of your friends are upper-class. Exactly the same goes for lower and middle. YET ... I have personally witnessed plenty of discrimination in regards to class. There are many upper-class people who judge the lower-class purely based on where they live and how much money they have before they even know them. The same goes for how lower-class can perceive upper-class. My point here is a reminder not to take your so-called 'class' too seriously. After all, we are all humans. This won't be relevant to everybody, but if it is to you, perhaps ask yourself why?

THE MIND – PART 3

I wanted to remind you how easy it is to latch onto thoughts as they arise, because I believe understanding this can change your life completely. We believe these thoughts and buy into them most of the time, because it's our mind, right?

Why would we not believe the things that come up? The thing is, sometimes our thoughts don't need to be taken seriously. Sometimes, they are just plain wrong. We have spoken about anxiety, and alongside this, you have paranoia, self-doubt, schizophrenia and suicide. All of the above are caused by an initial thought that was taken so seriously, it completely controlled us. I hope this puts into perspective how thoughts can really f**k us up!

Here's the good part. There is a solution. Next time a thought pops up that is scary or unpleasant, simply become aware of it and inject it with your 'SERIOUS ANTIDOTE' just like we discussed before. I felt a reminder of this was necessary, because I had to remind myself constantly before I really learnt not to take my thoughts so seriously.

BEING APPROPRIATE

Being 'appropriate' is basically caging the real you. Appropriate is what others expect you to be like. When you are a child and you let out a fart by accident at the dinner table, you are told, "That is very inappropriate! Never do that again." Little do your parents know that it just slipped out and couldn't be helped. Yet from now on, every time you need to fart at the dinner table, you will remember this and will hold it in, which can be very uncomfortable as we all know. This is just one example of how society and the people around you tell you what's appropriate and inappropriate. Now some things are clearly inappropriate. Groping someone you don't know at all is just plain wrong and an invasion of privacy. BUT ... if you want to sing your heart out on the train or burp in a restaurant, then I dare you to do it! Break down that big appropriate wall and do what you really want to do, when you want to do it. Show all them serious, appropriate people what it's like to really live and be free from the shackles of having to be appropriate!

EVERYTHING

We can afford to be less serious about literally everything!
Think now of the things that you take most seriously.
Write five of them down. Perhaps it would be:

1.   Your Career.
2.   Your Image.
3.   Your Ambitions.
4.   Your Diet.
5.   Your Relationship.

All of these do require a certain level of seriousness, but if
you can at least extinguish a good portion of how seriously
you take them, then you will feel a great weight being
lifted from your shoulders.
For example, by realising you take your relationship too
seriously, you will begin to inject a natural excitement and
freshness back into it, because you are back to being the
playful, fun person your partner originally loved.
So, think about your own seriousness and think how you
can change it?

Conclusion

Well, here we are. At the end of our journey to a less serious and more enjoyable life. I hope by now you have experienced and understood some of the benefits that a less serious perspective of life can have. Don't let this be the last time you pick up this book.

If you ever catch yourself becoming a little bit serious again, then come back to this and remind yourself of just how unserious life can be.

You will continue to face challenges throughout your life, this is for certain, yet with your new understanding you won't take these challenges so seriously. By doing so, you will be calmer, which will actually help you overcome your challenges with a stress-free, clear head.

Being less serious will bring out your natural playful side which we all have in us. It's basically our inner child which never really went away. That playfulness is attractive to most, because, after all the work and stress and other chores are done, we love nothing more than to relax and have a play.

The truth is you can do these things most of the time. There is no need for stress, it is completely useless to us. We create it when things don't go our way and we get all serious. Instead, just relax, get it done, make it fun if you can and return to the true playful you.

Imagine you go on two dates with either a boy or a girl. The first date is very serious about everything. They have already worked out exactly what to say, they talk about politics and the news and they order a salad and a mineral water because they are on a strict diet.

The second one goes with the flow. They ask you interesting and imaginative questions, they tease you from time to time, they express themselves fully and they order the burger on special which you have a bite of, because it looks so tasty!

Which one are you going to ask on that second date? We can all afford to be less serious and we can all reap the benefits. I challenge you to find every opportunity to let out your expressive, playful and true self.

Things will still seem serious sometimes, but you can pick up this book and re-evaluate just how serious it really is. Thank you for reading. Now go and do something crazy!